HIS STORY

(Volume 1)

A Simple Look Through

GENESIS

Carmel Carberry

www.gardenlandministries.org
https://carmelcarberry.wordpress.com

Copyright © 2021 Carmel Carberry. All rights reserved
This book is updated from the authors original work in 2018

Produced by Amazon Digital Services
IBSN: 9798739318664

Images by John and Carmel Carberry, and Georgie Carberry.
Used with permission. All rights reserved.

Unless otherwise indicated, all Scripture quotations are taken from *the Holy Bible*, New Living Translation, copyright 1996, 2004. Used by permission of Tyndale House Publishers Inc., Wheaton, Illinois. All rights reserved.

Other Scripture quotations taken from the following versions of the *Holy Bible*:

New International Version (NIV) ~ *Holy Bible, New International Version®, NIV® Copyright © 1973, 1978, 1984, 2011 by Biblica, Inc.® Used by permission. All rights reserved worldwide*

The Message (MSG) ~ *Copyright © 1993, 1994, 1995, 1996, 2000, 2001, 2002 by Eugene H. Peterson*

Amplified Bible (AMP) ~ *Copyright © 1954, 1958, 1962, 1964, 1965, 1987 by The Lockman Foundation*

King James Version (KJV) ~ *By Public Domain*

New King James Version (NKJV) ~ *The Holy Bible, New King James Version Copyright © 1982 by Thomas Nelson, Inc.*

Good News Translation (GNT) ~ *Copyright © 1992 by American Bible Society*

New Life Version (NLV) ~ *Copyright © 1969 by Christian Literature International*

New Century Version (NCV) ~ *Copyright © 2005 by Thomas Nelson, Inc.*

Author's Note

Over the years, many people have told me that they find The Bible difficult to read, and that often they do not understand it. Yet there is such wonderful wisdom and wise counsel within its pages.

With this in mind, I hope that this series will help readers to understand a bit more from the wealth of knowledge that The Scriptures contain and begin to enjoy them.

I pray that this insight helps readers to know deeper The One whom The Bible points to: The God of Love who is seen through His Son Jesus, who came for you.

ACKNOWLEDGMENTS

Special thanks to
JOHN CARBERRY
for his wisdom and insight always;
especially in helping to provide
answers and thoughts to
consider, which are recorded
in Section 6 of this book.

*We would like to take this opportunity to
acknowledge a dear friend and mentor,
Cliff Hughes, who blessed us and our
Ministry many times over the years.
Our friends help guide us and shape
the people we become, thank you Cliff.
With our love and prayers.
John & Carmel x*

Your love, LORD,
reaches to the heavens,
Your faithfulness
to the skies.

Psalm 36:5 (NIV)

CONTENTS

SIMPLE OVERVIEW OF THE BIBLE		Page 2
Section 1	Genesis chapters 1-5	Page 10
Section 2	Genesis chapters 6-11	Page 18
Section 3	Genesis chapters 12-25	Page 26
Section 4	Genesis chapters 25-36	Page 38
Section 5	Genesis chapters 37-50	Page 46
Section 6	Questions and Answers	Page 54
Section 7	List & Timeline (for reference)	Page 62
Personal study notes		Page 68
About The Author and 'Gardenland'		Page 86
Encouragements and Prayer		Page 90

JESUS SAID:

"Are you tired? Worn out?
Burned out on religion? Come to Me.
Get away with Me and you'll recover your life.
I'll show you how to take a real rest.
Walk with Me and work with Me—
watch how I do it. Learn the unforced
rhythms of grace. I won't lay anything heavy
or ill-fitting on you. Keep company with Me
and you'll learn to live freely and lightly.

Taken from Matthew 11:28-28 (MSG)

SIMPLE OVERVIEW OF THE BIBLE

The OLD TESTAMENT consists of the first 39 books of The Bible. The name 'Testament' refers to a covenant (meaning a 'binding agreement' or 'promise') that has been made between God and man.

In the Old Testament, we see that God made promises to men of faith who lived long ago; and God remains faithful to His promises *(for example: Adam ~ Genesis 1:26-30 // Noah ~ Genesis 9:11 // Abraham ~ Genesis 12:1-3 // Moses ~ Exodus 19-24 // David ~ 2 Samuel 5:7)*

The Bible begins by telling us that God is the Creator of all life and the whole universe. It introduces us to the first human beings and their descendants, with an emphasis on Abraham, his son Isaac, and his grandson Jacob.... who fathered the nation Israel.

Then the story of the Israelites' exodus from Egypt is told, and the development of Israel as a nation, including a variety of laws that were given to them.

There are also accounts of Leaders and Kings who ruled over the people and the many up and downs that this small but enduring nation faced over the centuries.

God spoke through many prophets to this nation with guidance, encouragements, and warnings, but also gave a message for the whole world through them that He would send an eternal Saviour who would come for all mankind.

The Bible as a whole shows mankind's need for a Saviour, and it prophesies about Him throughout the Old Testament.

Many rituals in the Old Testament (OT) have symbolism attached to them that act as a pointer towards the promised 'Christ' (*meaning 'Anointed One'*). Many of the Biblical heroes are also like 'types' or 'shadows' that point to Him.

~~~~~

Jesus is The Christ who is revealed in the New Testament (NT).
Some Bible references to consider: Isaiah 9:6 (OT) //
Matthew 1:23 / Matt 22:36-40 / Rom 10:4 (NT)

~~~~~

The NEW TESTAMENT is composed of the remaining 27 books of The Bible.

As we saw previously, the name 'Testament' refers to a covenant (agreement or promise) made between God and man. Ultimately, the fulfilment of all the Old Testament laws and prophets has come through Jesus *(Matt 5:17).*

The New Testament shows us the NEW COVENANT, which is the Eternal Covenant of Grace that God has made through the complete and finished work of Jesus at The Cross, and by His Resurrection *(Rom 3:23-26 / Heb 1:1-3).*

The New Testament tells us how Jesus accomplished salvation for all mankind and showed us God's Heart *(John 1:18).* We see the Love and Grace of God revealed in His Life and Ministry, as shown in The Gospels (Matthew, Mark, Luke, and John).

Then the New Testament pages tell us about the pouring out of God's Holy Spirit, the growth and impact of the early church (Acts) and records letters written by The Apostles to encourage and instruct the early church, and the generations that followed.

We can glean great wisdom, encouragement and insight through all of these, which lead us to 'Good News' ~ The Revelation of God's Love and Grace through Christ, God's One and Only Son *(John 3:16-17)*

The following pages list the names of the 66 books that make up the Bible as we know it. Then, Genesis chapter one is shared from the New Living Vision, followed by sections one to five which offer a simple look through the whole book of GENESIS (This Bible-book is part of a group often known as 'The Pentateuch', or 'Torah', or 'Books of The Law').

Bible Books Overview

Old Testament book titles with brief, simplistic description

- GENESIS – Creation, Noah, Tower of Babel, Abraham, Isaac, Jacob; Joseph and the beginning of the nation Israel
- EXODUS – Israel escape from Egypt after being held in slavery
- LEVITICUS – The Law of Moses is given to Israel
- NUMBERS – Israel wanders through the desert
- DEUTERONOMY – a continued history of Israel
- JOSHUA – an account of Israel entering the Promised Land
- JUDGES – a time of no clear leadership (inc. story of Samson)
- RUTH – a story of romance and family loyalty
- 1&2 SAMUEL – the first Kings of Israel (inc. King David)
- 1&2 KINGS – stories of success and failure
- 1&2 CHRONICLES – a history of David's royal line
- EZRA – the nation returns to the land God promised
- NEHEMIAH – the rebuilding of Jerusalem
- ESTHER – a queen acts bravely to save her people
- JOB – a man is restored after a time of suffering
- PSALMS – poems and songs, written and sung for God
- PROVERBS – wise advice (generally from Solomon)
- ECCLESIASTES – life is meaningless without God
- SONG OF SONGS – a story of adoring love
- ISAIAH – warnings; future hope; promises of a Saviour
- JEREMIAH – God is on The Throne, despite bad times
- LAMENTATIONS – a nation recalls their suffering
- EZEKIEL – visions of heaven; messages to nations
- DANIEL – a story of faith through difficult times
- HOSEA – a story of disloyalty
- JOEL – mercy triumphs over judgement
- AMOS – a call for justice
- OBADIAH – God defeats His enemies

- JONAH – God's message delivers a city
- MICAH – a crisis followed by hope
- NAHUM – God is to be honoured
- HABAKKUK – life doesn't always make sense
- ZEPHANIAH – the day of God's promise is near
- HAGGAI – a call to get ready
- ZECHARIAH – promises of restoration
- MALACHI – the promised Saviour is coming

New Testament book titles with a brief, simplistic description

- The Gospel of MATTHEW – Looking at Jesus: The Saviour is here!
- The Gospel of MARK – Looking at Jesus: Healer and Deliverer
- The Gospel of LUKE – Looking at Jesus: He came for all people
- The Gospel of JOHN – Looking at Jesus: God is with us
- ACTS – Christ ascends to heaven; the Holy Spirit is poured out on all flesh; Jesus' message of God's mercy begins to be proclaimed to all the earth
- ROMANS – Christ, the hope of all nations
- 1&2 CORINTHIANS – instruction on how to confront problems
- GALATIANS – Christ has set you free, stay free!
- EPHESIANS – a picture of who we are in Christ
- PHILIPPIANS – instruction to follow the example of Jesus
- COLOSSIANS – a description of the completeness of Jesus
- 1&2 THESSALONIANS – encouragement for today and forever
- 1&2 TIMOTHY – instruction on how to manage a difficult task
- TITUS – encouragement to finish the job
- PHILEMON – encouragement to forgive a fellow believer
- HEBREWS – the message of the New Covenant, sealed by Jesus
- JAMES – instruction on how to live a life of faith
- 1&2 PETER – encouragement to keep believing
- 1&2&3 JOHN – stay focused on God's love and truth
- JUDE – encouragement to stay in faith
- REVELATION – A vision of The Heavenly King Jesus; a look at world events from Heaven's perspective; a promise that God is making all things new!

Genesis Chapter 1 (NLV)

^{1} In the beginning God made from nothing the heavens and the earth. ^{2} The earth was an empty waste and darkness was over the deep waters. And the Spirit of God was moving over the top of the waters. ^{3} Then God said, "Let there be light," and there was light. ^{4} God saw that the light was good. He divided the light from the darkness. ^{5} Then God called the light day, and He called the darkness night. There was evening and there was morning, one day. ^{6} Then God said, "Let there be an open space between the waters. Let it divide waters from waters." ^{7} God made the open space, and divided the waters under the open space from the waters above the open space. And it was so. ^{8} Then God called the open space Heaven. There was evening and there was morning, the second day.

^{9} Then God said, "Let the waters under the heavens be gathered into one place. Let the dry land be seen." And it was so. ^{10} Then God called the dry land Earth. He called the gathering of the waters Seas. And God saw that it was good. ^{11} Then God said, "Let plants grow from the earth, plants that have seeds. Let fruit trees grow on the earth that bring their kind of fruit with their own seeds." And it was so. ^{12} Plants grew out of the earth, giving their own kind of seeds. Trees grew with their fruit, and their kind of seeds. And God saw that it was good. ^{13} There was evening and there was morning, the third day.

^{14} Then God said, "Let there be lights in the open space of the heavens to divide day from night. Let them tell the days and years and times of the year. ^{15} Let them be lights in the open space of the heavens to give light on the earth." And it was so. ^{16} Then God made the two great lights, the brighter light to rule the day, and the smaller light to rule the night. He made the stars also. ^{17} God put them in the open space of the heavens to give light on the earth, ^{18} to rule the day and the night. He divided the light from the darkness. And God saw that it was good. ^{19} There was evening and there was morning, the fourth day.

20 Then God said, "Let the waters be full of living things. Let birds fly above the earth in the open space of the heavens." 21 God made the big animals that live in the sea, and every living thing that moves through the waters by its kind, and every winged bird after its kind. And God saw that it was good.

22 God wanted good to come to them, saying, "Give birth to many. Grow in number. Fill the waters in the seas. Let birds grow in number on the earth." 23 There was evening and there was morning, the fifth day.

24 Then God said, "Let the earth bring into being living things after their kind: Cattle and things that move upon the ground, and wild animals of the earth after their kind." And it was so. 25 Then God made the wild animals of the earth after their kind, and the cattle after their kind, and every thing that moves upon the ground after its kind. And God saw that it was good.

26 Then God said, "Let Us make man like Us and let him be head over the fish of the sea, and over the birds of the air, and over the cattle, and over all the earth, and over every thing that moves on the ground." 27 And God made man in His own likeness. In the likeness of God He made him. He made both male and female.

28 And God wanted good to come to them, saying, "Give birth to many. Grow in number. Fill the earth and rule over it. Rule over the fish of the sea, over the birds of the sky, and over every living thing that moves on the earth."

29 Then God said, "See, I have given you every plant that gives seeds that is on the earth, and every tree that has fruit that gives seeds. They will be food for you. 30 I have given every green plant for food to every animal of the earth, and to every bird of the sky, and to every thing that moves on the earth that has life." And it was so.

31 God saw all that He had made and it was very good. There was evening and there was morning, the sixth day.

Section One

The Beginning

The name 'Genesis' means 'origins' or 'beginnings. It is believed to have been written down by Moses (who lived 1393 B.C - 1273 B.C.). This first Book of The Bible begins by telling us that ***God created*** the heavens and the earth (Gen 1:1). The full account of creation can be seen across Genesis chapters 1-2.

Since Moses was not born at the time of Creation, it is believed that God spoke to Moses and led him to write as he did. It seems that God gave just enough information that He deemed important to be recorded, so that it could be passed down from generation to generation and people could learn from it.

Genesis also teaches a lot about relationships, particularly the relationship that God desires with mankind ~ the 'pinnacle of His creation' (*meaning the 'highpoint' or 'highlight' of His creation* ~ see Gen 1:26-31).

God made man from the dust of the ground into which He breathed life and it became a human being (Gen 2:7). This was the first man, Adam. God also gave Adam a special helper, whom Adam named as Eve in Gen 3:20.

She was a companion and an equal to Adam ~ even made from part of Adam's body [his rib] (Gen 2:22-24). She was made a special and perfect helper (a gift of grace from God).

Basic summary of the order of Creation

Day 1	LIGHT APPEARED (so there was light and darkness/day and night)
Day 2	SKY AND WATER ('waters separated')
Day 3	LAND AND SEAS ('waters gathered', land revealed); VEGETATION grew on the land
Day 4	SUN, MOON, AND STARS (to govern the day/night, and to mark seasons/days/years)
Day 5	FISH AND BIRDS (fish to fill the waters and birds to fill the sky)
Day 6	ANIMALS (land animals to fill the earth) MAN AND WOMAN (to care for the earth, fill the earth and to fellowship with God)
Day 7	GOD RESTED and said that all He had made was very good

Genesis tells us that God walked with Adam as a friend as well as his God and Creator, but the 'fall of man' (man's disobedience to God's instruction ~ Gen 3:1-7) brought fear and mistrust into the previously close relationship mankind had with God. Adam and Eve became afraid for the first time (Gen 3:8).

It was this event that brought sin into the world and ultimately affected the whole of creation, even to the present day (Rom 8:22).

Despite this bad news, **God had Good News to tell of a Saviour** who would one day come into the world and restore the relationship between God and man (John 3:16-17).

God spoke about this to Adam and Eve, when He prophesied that the *'seed of the woman'* (speaking of one of Eve's descendants ~ Jesus) who would one day *'bruise the serpent's head'* (speaking of the devil's head ~ Gen 3:15).

God also said that the evil one would strike the offspring (Jesus) ~ *this was a reference to The Cross where Jesus would ultimately pay for sin for all mankind.*

Continuing to consider Genesis 3, we see that after the fall of man, God sent Adam and Eve out of the Garden of Eden. But this was to protect them, not reject them.

For, at the moment of the 'fall' (Gen 3), sin and death began to affect all of creation.

God knew that it was not good for mankind to live for all time in a fallen state, therefore Adam and Eve were kept away from the 'Tree of Eternal Life' (in the garden) so that mankind did not eternally live in a sin filled world, with all its sickness and suffering forever.

But they did still have long lives (Adam lived 930 years according to Gen 5:3-5). God still spoke to them and He still intervened in man's existence.

However, until Jesus came, the 'man to God relationship' could not be the perfect one they had originally known.

Unfortunately, mankind frequently refused to listen to God's voice across the years, which led to many tragedies among the human race in the times that followed.

For example, the well-known story of two of Adam and Eve's children is recorded for us in Genesis 4, where Cain became jealous of his brother Abel and murdered him.

Prior to this happening, God spoke to Cain to warn him not to allow sin to consume his heart, but he refused God's advice (Gen 4:6-7).

And yet, God showed grace to Cain even after the event, offering him protection from others who might want to kill him later on in revenge.

It can sometimes be missed when reading the Old Testament, that in fact God shows amazing grace often!

When we come to verse Genesis 4:16 we see an interesting thing...that Cain chose to leave God's presence despite the grace he was shown. Basically, Cain had developed a hardened heart by persistently refusing to listen to God's voice.

If he had chosen to listen, he could have reversed this hardening, but instead he walked away from God.... here we see an example of mankind walking away from God, not the other way around.

God does not forsake us ~ we see that in the New Testament ~ but love and faithfulness has always been His real heart *(compare the heart of God in Old and New Testament Bible verses below)*:

Hebrews 13:5b (New Testament)
God has said, "I will never fail you. I will never abandon you."

Jeremiah 29:11 (Old Testament)
"For I know the plans I have for you," says the LORD.
"They are plans for good and not for disaster, to give you a future and a hope.

Cain's family is spoken of in Gen 4:16-24. The Bible gives insight during this record of his descendants, that mankind was beginning to take God's grace and mercy as an approval of sinful actions.

We see this in the selfish reaction of Cain's great grandson Lamech, who chooses to kill another man but assumes that God will condone his action because of the kindness God had showed to Cain previously (Gen 4:23-24).

At the end of Genesis chapter 4 (verses 25-26), we see that Adam and Eve have another son whom they name Seth, and when he grows up, he in turn has a son named Enosh. In these verses we also see a beautiful phrase saying, ***'then men began to call on the name of The Lord"***.

Genesis chapter 5 goes on to list the ten generations of people that came from Adam through to the birth of Noah (like a family tree growing and leading out from the first man, created by God in His Love).

Section Two

Noah and The Flood

As we move into chapter 6 of The Book of Genesis, we see the human race multiplying out from the initial families originally born from Adam and Eve.

Then, Genesis 6:2 includes a mysterious phrase *'the sons of God'* (which many believe to be a reference to angels or spiritual beings {probably fallen angels} considering similar references found in Job 1:6 / Job 2:1).

Whoever they were, we are told in Genesis 6:2-4 that they procreated with some of the *'daughters of men'* (female descendants of mankind) which led to a set of 'hybrid' offspring who became incredible giants known as the 'Nephilim' in The Bible (Gen 6:4).

This union and offspring do not appear to be something that God intended for mankind, as verses 5 to 6 say that it was something that 'grieved Him'.

This chapter goes on to tell us that mankind was doing 'evil upon evil', to one another and to God's creative order, causing chaos upon the face of the earth.

He did not want mankind to continue on this destructive path of evil forever, which had the potential to wipe everything out, including mankind himself.

However, one man caught God's attention, the man Noah ~ who The Bible says was 'just in nature', 'walked with God', and 'received His Grace' (Gen 6:8-9).

It was this man that God spoke to and instructed to build an Ark, in order to preserve a remnant of mankind who could grow and increase again after The Great Flood which covered the whole earth (Gen 7).

God also told Noah to take animals aboard to save as much of His creation as possible, and allow mankind to begin afresh upon the earth that He had created for them to live upon, care for and enjoy.

As we go into chapters 7-10 we see how Noah obeyed God, despite how odd it must have seemed to him at the time. Noah and his family (along with the animals that he saved) ultimately lived inside this great ship to overcome the storm and flood.

The Ark kept its inhabitants safe as God promised; so that they could begin afresh and repopulate the earth.

God gave a sign to Noah and his descendants to mark a covenant (i.e. an agreement/promise) that He would never flood the earth again: He placed a *rainbow in the sky*, which continues to be a reminder today, of His promise to Noah and all mankind (Gen 9:11-16).

It is also interesting that in Genesis 9:3 there is a word from God that from this point in history both meat and vegetation could be part of mankind's diet. Perhaps the environment changed at this point due to the effect of the flood?

Perhaps the vegetation no longer held the fullness of nutrition that was originally in the Garden of Eden that had once met man's needs completely? Note: these are THOUGHTS to consider.

The Tower of Babel.

As we continue to look at Genesis 10, we are shown that nations developed over the course of centuries from Noah's descendants, who all spoke one language initially (Gen 11:1).

However, moving into Chapter 11, we see the Bible's explanation for the onset of multiple languages when people dispersed across the earth, as told in the story of The Tower of Babel (Gen 11:1-9)

Basically, it seems that the people generally became arrogant and proud, and intended to settle in one place, and build a mighty tower.

Perhaps the danger here was the immense ability these people had as they worked together but would it be used for good or evil? Only God knows the depths of people's hearts.

It is worth considering that God gave Adam and Eve an instruction at the beginning of Genesis, for their offspring to *fill the earth* and to *rule over it wisely* (Gen 1:28).

However, at Babel mankind was building a tower: a) in a vain attempt to reach heaven through their own efforts and b) trying to avoid being scattered across the earth (Gen 11:4).

Therefore, God confused their speech into different languages, which brought an end to man's self-serving work at this point, so that mankind *did* scatter and begin to fill the earth with their descendants (Gen 11:8-9).

The following verses of chapter 11 lead into another list of generations that followed the event at Babel, through to the man 'Abram' who is later called 'Abraham' by God.

We will continue to take a glimpse at his life and his family in the next section, when we journey through the chapters that introduce us to the 'patriarchs' (which basically means the founding fathers of the family line) who formed the nation ***Israel****.

This is important in the Bible because Jesus came to earth to live in human form (John 1:14) born from the line of ***Abraham and his descendants**** with the purpose to save the whole world (Matt 1:1-17 / John 3:16-17).

His story is linked to this line of genealogy, and from the beginning all that is written in the pages of The Bible is to show us our need for a Saviour and lead us to Him!

Matthew 1:1-17 (NCV)

**¹This is the family history of Jesus Christ.
He came from the family of David,
and David came from the family of Abraham.**

*² Abraham was the father of Isaac.
Isaac was the father of Jacob.
Jacob was the father of Judah and his brothers.
³ Judah was the father of Perez and Zerah.
(Their mother was Tamar.)
Perez was the father of Hezron.
Hezron was the father of Ram.
⁴ Ram was the father of Amminadab.
Amminadab was the father of Nahshon.
Nahshon was the father of Salmon.
⁵ Salmon was the father of Boaz.
(Boaz's mother was Rahab.)
Boaz was the father of Obed.
(Obed's mother was Ruth.)
Obed was the father of Jesse.
⁶ Jesse was the father of King David.*

*David was the father of Solomon.
(Solomon's mother had been Uriah's wife.)
⁷ Solomon was the father of Rehoboam.
Rehoboam was the father of Abijah.
Abijah was the father of Asa.
⁸ Asa was the father of Jehoshaphat.
Jehoshaphat was the father of Jehoram.
Jehoram was the ancestor of Uzziah.*

⁹ Uzziah was the father of Jotham.
Jotham was the father of Ahaz.
Ahaz was the father of Hezekiah.
¹⁰ Hezekiah was the father of Manasseh.
Manasseh was the father of Amon.
Amon was the father of Josiah.
¹¹ Josiah was the grandfather of Jehoiachin[and his brothers.
(This was at the time that the people were taken to Babylon.)

¹² After they were taken to Babylon:
Jehoiachin was the father of Shealtiel.
Shealtiel was the grandfather of Zerubbabel.
¹³ Zerubbabel was the father of Abiud.
Abiud was the father of Eliakim.
Eliakim was the father of Azor.
¹⁴ Azor was the father of Zadok.
Zadok was the father of Akim.
Akim was the father of Eliud.
¹⁵ Eliud was the father of Eleazar.
Eleazar was the father of Matthan.
Matthan was the father of Jacob.
¹⁶ Jacob was the father of Joseph.
Joseph was the husband of Mary,
and Mary was the mother of Jesus.
Jesus is called the Christ.

¹⁷ So there were fourteen generations from Abraham to David.
And there were fourteen generations from David
until the people were taken to Babylon.
And there were fourteen generations from the time when
the people were taken to Babylon until Christ was born.

Section Three

Abraham and his family

As we move into chapter 12 of The Book of Genesis, we can gain an insight into the lives of ***The Patriarchs*** (the founding fathers of the nation of Israel ~ ***Abraham, Isaac and Jacob***).

Here we are told about a man named 'Abram' (later his name is changed to 'Abraham'), who was one of the sons of a man named Terah ~ a tenth generation descendent of Noah (Gen 11:31-32). Abram was married to a woman called Sarai, who was his half-sister.

In Genesis 12:1-3, God speaks to Abram calling him to leave his home country and travel to a land that He promises to show Abram; God promised to bless him and make him become a 'great nation'.

As we proceed through the next chapters, we read a number of stories about Abram. The Bible appears to deem it important to record these stories for our information and for us to be able to learn from.

When Abram was 75 years old he began to travel as God instructed, along with his wife Sarai ~ but he also took his nephew Lot ~ and all their servants and livestock.

When a famine broke out in Canaan, they travelled south to Egypt, but Abram was afraid of the Egyptians, so he instructed Sarai to tell the Pharaoh that she was his 'sister' but not to tell him that she was also Abram's wife (thinking this might protect them).

Since Abram had not informed Pharaoh that Sarai was his wife, Pharaoh took her to be his own. However, once he learned the truth, he immediately released Sarai unharmed and sent Abram and his wife on their way.

Here is an example of God showing grace to Abram, even though he lied out of fear of Pharaoh and his men; but God kept His promise to look after them despite their imperfections.

But *in faith*, wherever Abram went, he continued to worship God (Gen 13:3-4).

Over a period of time, the households of Abram and Lot became too big to stay together. So, Lot and his household decided to go east and live in the Jorden Valley (towards Sodom); and Abram and his household went to live in Canaan (Gen 13:10-13).

Then, God repeats His promise to Abram to bless him as he proceeds toward Hebron (Gen 13:14-18).

As we move on into Genesis 14, we read about an occasion where Lot was captured by the people of Sodom, and Abram came to his rescue.

The king of Sodom met with Abram, but he did not make a treaty with the king; he simply gave the king what was legally his and then ensured that anything stolen from Lot was returned.

We are also told in Genesis 14 about a mysterious figure being present at this meeting alongside Abram: someone called *'Melchizedek ~ King of Salem' (meaning 'King of Righteousness / Prince of Peace').*

> *For further study, compare the names and details associated with Melchizedek which also appear in Hebrews chapter 7 (in the New Testament) where Jesus is spoken about in the same way, being called Priest of The Most High; King of Righteousness and Prince of Peace*

In these verses *'Melchizedek'* is also called *'Priest of The Most High'* who brought *'bread and wine'*. He blessed Abram, who then chose to give a tenth of everything to Melchizedek (Gen 14:18-20).

> *Also compare the above with references about Jesus in the New Testament, for example: Matt 26:26-28 / Heb 7:1-3*

Moving into Genesis 15-16, God speaks again to Abram in a vision to reassure him about the truth of His promise to provide a land for his descendants, who would be 'as numerous as the stars' (Gen 15:5).

Then there is a beautiful phrase that we can all take to heart: *'he believed in The Lord and God counted it to him as righteousness'* (Gen 15:6 KJV).

God also spoke to Abram of a time when his descendants would be slaves in Egypt, but one day they would move into the land that God was giving them.

As Abram and Sarai tried to make sense of all of this, bearing in mind that they did not have children (and were getting older), they decided that Abram should have a child with Sarai's handmaid, called Hagar.

However, strife in the household followed when Hagar became pregnant, and this strife caused her to run away until God called her to return and promised to look after her and her child (Ishmael) too, along with his descendants (Gen 16).

Side-line note:
Within Old Testament pages we often see religious rituals that are difficult for us to understand in our modern world. The simplest way to consider them is that they had a spiritual purpose at that time (e.g. to seal an agreement in the context of that period of history); and often they were a reflection or pointer to the coming of The Saviour who would pay for all sin for all time. For example:

Consider Hebrews 6:13-18 (NLV)
[13] *.... there was God's promise to Abraham: God took an oath in His own name, since there was no one greater to swear by, [14] that He would bless Abraham again and again, and give him a son and make him the father of a great nation of people. [15] Then Abraham waited patiently until finally God gave him a son, Isaac, just as He had promised. [16] When a man takes an oath, he is calling upon someone greater than himself to force him to do what he has promised or to punish him if he later refuses to do it; the oath ends all argument about it.*

17 God also bound Himself with an oath, so that those He promised to help would be perfectly sure and never need to wonder whether He might change His plans. 18 He has given us both His promise and His oath, two things we can completely count on, for it is impossible for God to tell a lie. Now all those who flee to Him to save them can take new courage when they hear such assurances from God; now they can know without doubt that He will give them the salvation He has promised them.

Thirteen years later, God gave Abram a new name: 'Abraham' which means 'father of many nations' (Gen 17:5).

Sarai also received a new name from God at this time. She became 'Sarah' and God repeated His promised that she would bear a son to Abraham and he would also receive God's blessing (Gen 17:15-16).

Abraham wondered how he could possible father a son at 100 years old with his wife who was 90 years old (Gen 17:17-21). As a sign of His covenant (agreement/promise), God gave instructions to Abraham regarding circumcision (Gen 17:9-12 / 23-27).

<u>Heavenly Visitors</u>

One day when Abraham was sitting at the entrance to his tent he saw what appeared to be three men approaching him. These men shone with God's presence, so Abraham ran to greet them and bowed before them (Gen 18:1-8).

One of the 'men' *(who are considered to be 'heavenly visitors')* said to Abraham that he would return the following year by which time Sarah would have a son.

Overhearing this Sarah laughed at the idea, but the visitor responded by saying is anything too difficult for God? (Gen 18:14)

After a meal, Abraham and his heavenly visitors walked together to a high peak to view the 'cities of the plain' and discussed the future of Sodom and Gomorrah.

Abraham's nephew lived in Sodom, so God chose to talk with Abraham about the cities and gave warnings of things to come (Gen 18:17-33).

As we read on, The Bible makes us aware that appalling things were happening in the two infamous cities, therefore God decided that these places needed to be destroyed to prevent further calamity upon the earth.

In chapter 19, we see that Lot listened to the warnings God gave, so he and his family left the area before the city's destruction.

When we look at Genesis chapter 20, we see that once again Abraham does not inform the king of the next place he travels to that Sarah is his wife.

We need to remember that the people we see recorded in The Bible were ordinary people who sometimes made mistakes, ***but God looks at the heart and He delights when people have faith and show trust in Him.***

God is gracious, so when those who put their hope in Him 'mess up' He still seeks to guide them in His mercy and still bring good out of potentially bad situations. This is why it is good to listen to Him *(consider Romans 8:26-28 the New Testament)*.

So, 'King Abimelech' in his ignorance takes Sarah into his own house but God speaks to him in a dream to warn him that she is another man's wife (Gen 20:1-7). Understanding this, he returns her to her rightful husband Abraham, who prays for Abimelech and his household (Gen 20:8-18).

We hear about Abimelech again later on when a disagreement develops among some of his men concerning a well that Abraham built.

They go on to make a treaty and resolve the dispute. Abraham then remained there and planted a grove in a place called 'Beersheba', and honoured God (Gen 21:22-34).

God's promise to Abraham that Sarah herself would bear a son to him (Gen 17:21) was ultimately fulfilled when he was a hundred years old. The child was named 'Isaac' which means 'laughter' (Gen 21:1-7).

Unfortunately, strife broke out in the household when Sarah saw Ishmael (Abrahams's son through Hagar) mocking Isaac her son (Gen 21:8-13).

In her anger, Sarah insisted that Ishmael and his mother were sent away by Abraham, and that Ishmael would not share in Isaacs's inheritance, which distressed Abraham.

But God reassured Abraham that Isaac would have descendants as He had promised (Gen 21:12), *and* that Ishmael too would have descendants who would become a nation (Gen 21:9-13)

Hagar and Ishmael were given supplies and sent away as Sarah insisted. The mother and boy wandered in the wilderness of Beersheba, until their water ran out, then Hagar began to cry.

She sent Ishmael a little further way from her (in her despair) and he too began to cry in anguish. But God spoke to Hagar and instructed her to go and comfort the boy.

God told her that they both would live, and that Ishmael would become a great nation as He had promised Abraham. With that *word from God,* a well of water appeared and their lives were saved.

The boy grew to become an archer and lived in Paran. Ultimately, he found a wife from the country of Egypt (Gen 21:14-21).

The offering of Isaac

As we move on into Genesis chapter 22, we see the account of God calling Abraham to 'offer up' his promised son Isaac. This command must have puzzled Abraham greatly

Yet, *he remained faithful and believed* that somehow God would still keep His promises to him and look after the boy in a miraculous way.

However, as we read through the verses of the account, it is clear that Abraham did not know how God would help him and was often distressed.... but still he trusted God. It is an amazing example of faith despite the circumstances.

Abraham travelled three days to the mountain that God had told him to go to. Isaac walked with his father diligently and even carried the wood for the offering, since Abraham had told his son that 'God would provide' (Gen 22:8).

When it came time for Abraham to sacrifice his son, God immediately commanded Abraham *to stop* and said to him *'do not harm the boy!'* (Gen 22:12).

With that command, Abraham saw a ram caught by its horns in some undergrowth. God then told him to sacrifice the ram not his son and commends Abraham. God also gives another promise of descendants through Isaac along with the promise of prosperity.

After this Abraham went back to Beersheba (Gen 22:19).

The story of Abraham offering Isaac is a prophetic reflection of how God would one day offer His Own Son (Jesus) for the sins of the world.

God never intended Abraham to harm Isaac, but the Old Testament story points to a New Testament time where God The Father would give His One and Only Son so that all mankind could have the opportunity of a restored relationship with Him.

For further study, consider ~ John 3:16-17 / Rom 3:23-26 / 2 Cor 5:17-21 / Heb 11:17-19 ~ in the New Testament

~~~

Sarah lived to be 127 years old (Gen 23:1). When she died, Abraham buried her in the caves of The Patriarchs (the cave of Machpelah, near Hebron). Abraham bought this cave along with an adjacent field according to Genesis 23:1-20.

Isaac married a woman named Rebecca (Gen 24) and Abraham married again, to a woman named Keturah. Through Keturah, Abraham had six more sons (Gen 25:1-2).

The name that Abraham was given, meaning 'father of many nations' was fulfilled as his descendants grew, and did indeed become many nations.

Abraham was 175 years old when he died and was buried beside his wife Sarah in the cave of Machpelah by Isaac and Ishmael (Gen 25: 7-10).

Section Four

Issac and Jacob

Isaac and his family

As we move on further through Chapter 25 of Genesis, we read about Isaac's family. The Bible tells us that Isaac was 40 years old, when his wife Rebekah becomes pregnant with twins (Gen 25:21).

When Isaac and Rebecca's sons are born, the first son is followed moments later by his younger brother who was clutching at his elder brother's heel.

The name given to the first son was 'Esau' which means 'hair' (because Esau had hairy skin) while the name given to the second son was 'Jacob', which means 'heel-catcher' ~ the name can also mean 'one who deceives' (Gen 25:22-26).

When they grew up, Esau became a hunter and went out into the open countryside to hunt wild animals, while Jacob tended to stay at home.

One day, when Esau returned from one of his hunting trips hungry and tired, he demanded to be fed immediately when he saw Jacob preparing a red stew.

Jacob took advantage of the situation and bargained with Esau.

The older brother agreed to give up his 'inheritance' (or privileges) as first-born son to his younger brother in exchange for a bowl of the red stew.

After this, Esau also became known by a second name 'Edom' which means 'red' (Gen 25:29-34)

In chapter 26, we see Isaac and his family move to a place called Gerar. God speaks to Isaac promising to bless him and make his descendants 'as numerous as the stars of the sky' ~ just as He had promised Abraham, his father (Gen 26:1-6).

When some 'man-made' difficulties arise in Gerar, Isaac moves his family to Beersheba, where God speaks to Isaac again and reassures him that God's gracious promise still stands (despite some negative situations happening around Isaac).

In an act of faith and gratitude, Isaac built an Altar there to worship God (Gen 26:25). As life went on for Isaac, he took opportunities to make peace with people around him, but some difficulties remained unresolved (Gen 26:23-35). Eventually, when Isaac grew old, he came blind.

Jacob and Esau

One day, Isaac told his eldest son Esau to go on a hunting trip to bring some meat in order to a make a meal that they could share, where he would give a blessing to Esau (Gen 27:1-4).

However, while Esau is away, Rebecca helps Jacob to deceive his father into believing that Jacob is Esau. She prepares a separate meal and covers Jacob's arms with animal skins to feel like Esau's 'hairy' arms, and dresses Jacob in Esau's clothing (Gen 27:5-17).

Unknowingly, Isaac then gives his blessing to Jacob.

When Esau returns home to find out what has happened, he is furious. Jacob then fears his older brother, so runs away to his Uncle Laban's house in upper Mesopotamia.

Esau also decides to leave and travels to his Uncle Ishmael's house, where he settles and marries one of Ishmael's daughters (Gen 27:18 to Gen 28:9).

During Jacob's journey, he stops to rest and sleep, where he dreams of a stairway leading up to Heaven. He sees angels going up and down the stairway, and The Lord standing at the top.

God spoke in this dream/vision to say that He would look after Jacob and provide the same covenant (contract/agreement) that He had made with Abraham and Isaac. And God promises Jacob that his descendants will be as numerous as 'the dust of the earth' (Gen 28:10-14).

When he woke the next morning, Jacob took the stone on which he had rested his head overnight, poured oil over it and set it as a 'memorial stone' to honour God.

Jacob then named that place 'Bethel' (meaning 'house of God'). From his own heart, he also promised to give The Lord a tenth of everything he received from Him (Gen 28:15-22).

> ➢ *Side-line note ~ words have power and meaning*
> *The naming of places etc had deep meaning for people in The Bible. The Scriptures tell us that words are powerful and have life ~ they also tell us that Jesus is called **The Word of God,** and that God 'spoke' (i.e. used **'His Word'**) to create all things. For example:*

From Genesis 1:3 and John 1:1-3+14
God said, "Let there be light," and there was light... In the beginning The Word already existed......The Word was with God, and The Word was God......God created everything through Him....The Word became human and made His home among us [speaking of Jesus]. *He was full of unfailing love and faithfulness. And we have seen His glory, the glory of the Father's one and only Son.*

For further study also consider Proverbs 12:18+18:21 / Matthew 12:36-27 / Ephesians 4:29 / James 3:5b-8 / Hebrews 1:3 / John 1:17-18 / Hebrews 4:12-13 (in both the Old & New Testaments).

When Jacob arrived at Laban's house, he agreed to work for his uncle for seven years in exchange for being able to marry Laban's daughter, Rachel.

However, Laban deceived Jacob into marrying Rachel's older sister, Leah first. So, Jacob worked another seven years for Laban in order to marry Rachel too. Jacob went on to have eleven sons and a daughter (through his two wives and their maids).

The family prospered, but after a time, more difficulties in relationships caused Jacob and his family to leave Laban's house (Gen 29-31). God spoke to Jacob to return to Canaan (Gen 31:13), so he and his family began another journey.

Unknown to Jacob, Rachel stole a collection of Laban's 'idols' as she left her father's house {'idols' were small carvings meant to be miniature representations of false gods at the time} (Gen 31:19).

In an attempt to find his idols, Laban pursued Jacob into the desert, but failed to find the carvings (because Rebecca hid them), so the two men made peace with each other.

Jacob then erected a 'pillar of stone' as a 'witness' to a 'peaceful resolution' before God (Gen 31:45-54). After Laban left, Jacob encountered angels.

In his awe and wonder of God, he said, "this is God's camp!" and Jacob named that area 'Mehanaim' ~ meaning 'two camps (Gen 32:1-2).

Looking on through Genesis chapter 32, Jacob considered how he could avoid potential hostilities between Jacob's household and his bother Esau's household when they met. So, Jacob prepared gifts for his brother and sent them on in advance to appease him.

After settling his family into two separate camps, Jacob then spent the night at the river Jabbok, alone, in preparation for meeting his brother the following day (Gen 32:20-23).

During the night, Jacob met with God, who appeared like a man before him; Jacob wrestled with God and demanded a blessing from Him, which The Lord graciously gave.

God also gave Jacob a new name: 'Israel' (which means 'he struggles with God').

Jacob named that place Peniel (which means "face of God") and said, "I have seen God, yet He spared me!" (Gen 32:24-32).

> ➤ *Side-line note ~ **God shows more grace***

Here is another example of God's mercy being shown in even in the Old Testament, which can sometimes be easy to miss while reading chapters through. God loves to intervene and help people; despite times we might be wrestling. Even so, faith in God pleases Him and He longs to be gracious.

Isaiah 30:18 (GNT)
And yet the LORD is waiting to be merciful to you...because He always does what is right. Happy are those who put their trust in the LORD.

Moving into chapter 33, we see that when Jacob finally reunites with his older brother, Esau greets Jacob with open arms, and they are reconciled.

So, Jacob settles his family in Shechem to be near Esau's family (who had intermarried with the Canaanites and produced a tribe called the Edomites). For a time, they lived in peace.

Chapter 34 tells us that the peace was broken when Jacob's daughter, Dinah, was forced upon by a man from Shechem. Outraged by the attack, Jacob's sons plotted revenge on the man concerned (and his family).

The sons tell the man that he can marry Dinah, if he and all the male members of his household are circumcised, to which he agrees, but while they are recovering from the surgical procedure, Jacob's sons kill all the men.

Following this harrowing event, Jacobs's family had to go on the move again.

At this point, Jacob tells his family that they must get rid of any idols and false gods from the household (Gen 35:1-8).

Jacob recognized that God had been with him despite everything. Jacob knew that God alone answered him whenever he was distressed and only He truly deserves worship (Gen 35:3).

God spoke to Jacob reminding him of his new name 'Israel'; and (in grace and love) God reassured him that His blessing remained upon Jacob's descendants (Gen 35:9-11).

Eventually, Esau and Jacob came together again to bury Isaac when he died at 180 years old (Gen 35:28-29).

In chapter 36 the genealogy of the descendants of Esau is listed for future reference; the chapter also records how the tribe of the Edomites developed from their ancestor Esau.

Section Five

Joseph and his family

Joseph (part 1)

Moving on into chapter 37, we see Jacob's sons growing angry with Jacob's younger son Joseph (who was considered Jacob's favourite).

This came to a head when he gave Joseph a special coat that was multi-coloured; and intensified as Joseph told his brothers (and his parents) about prophetic dreams that he had, where all of them would one day bow before him (Gen 37:1-11).

In their jealously, the older brothers plotted to kill Joseph but then decide to sell him into slavery instead. They pretended to their father that Joseph was killed by a lion while they were out together in the wild.

To validate their deception, the brothers took Joseph's multi-coloured coat and tore it, then stained it with the blood of an animal, and showed it to their father Jacob (Gen 37:12-33).

Meanwhile, Joseph was sold as a slave to a man named Potiphar, who was a high-ranking official in Egypt (Gen 37:28+36).

Judah and Tamar

Whilst in the middle of Joseph's story, chapter 38 changes track to tell us some information regarding Judah, one of Joseph's older brothers (Jacob's older sons).

The Bible apparently deems this important enough to make a 'pit-stop' here in order to record this for our future reference.

Chapter 38 basically tells the account that Judah left his brothers for a while, and during his time away, he married a woman, and had two sons with her. When the time came for Judah to find a wife for his eldest son, he chose a young woman named Tamar.

The Bible tells us that the elder son turned out to be evil. After he died, Judah told his second son to look after Tamar, but he refused. Tamar was then sent back to her father's house (feeling rejected and ashamed).

When Judah's own wife died, he tried to find comfort by searching for a prostitute and ended up being comforted by Tamar by mistake. Later, Tamar had to prove to Judah that she was the woman he had spent the time with.

Once he realised the truth, he admitted his mistake and ensured that Tamar was provided for and not rejected or mistreated further. When she gave birth to twins, she named them Perez and Zerah.

This detour in the story records a change of heart in one of Joseph's brothers. It shows that Judah grew to recognize when he did something wrong, and sought to put it right. (Gen 38:26).

This leads to another example of amazing grace shown in the pages of The Bible, when it speaks of Judah with honour in later chapters (see Gen 49:8-12)

Joseph (part 2)

Returning to Joseph's story, Potiphar (who was Joseph's new master) treated him well. Potiphar saw that God was with his new slave, so he put Joseph in charge of the household. This in turn brought blessing upon the whole house, therefore his master was pleased (Gen 39:1-6).

However, Potiphar's wife saw how handsome Joseph was and began to make advances towards him. Being an honourable man, Joseph rejected her advances, but in revenge the wife lied and accused Joseph of trying to seduce her instead (Gen 39:6-18).

Believing his wife's story, Potiphar sends Joseph to prison. But Joseph remains faithful to God, and is given special responsibilities even within the prison itself, which prove to be a success for him (Gen 39:19-23).

As times goes on, Joseph builds up a reputation of being a dream interpreter. Eventually, Joseph is summoned by the Pharaoh of Egypt to interpret two particular dreams that were troubling the Pharaoh (Genesis 40-41).

As Joseph, interprets the dreams, he warns Pharaoh that a seven-year famine will strike Egypt after seven prosperous years have passed (Gen 41:29-32).

Joseph also suggests that during the seven good years prior to the famine, a portion of the abundance of grain should be collected and stored during the good years, and then be distributed fairly among the people during the famine (Gen 41:33-36).

Hearing Joseph's wisdom, Pharaoh promotes Joseph to be his highest official, and gives him the job of organizing food collection and storage in Egypt, in order to prepare for the future time of need (Gen 41:37-43).

When the famine came, it affected many lands around Egypt too. As other areas learnt of Egypt's storage and supply of grain, many people came from all around, looking to them for help and to purchase food from them.

Looking through chapters 42 to 47 ~ we see Jacob sending his sons to Egypt to buy food for his household when it became affected by the crisis. This leads to a powerful family reunion!

<u>Joseph (part 3)</u>

Joseph's brothers end up standing before Joseph in his official capacity in Egypt, but they did not recognise him. Joseph, however, immediately recognised them, even after all the years that had passed.

Initially, Joseph did not reveal his identity to his brothers. First Joseph tests them (with a variety of arranged situations) to see if their character has truly changed.

After sending them to jail for a short time, he then sends them back to Canaan insisting that they bring their youngest brother Benjamin with them.

On their return Joseph tests his brothers' reactions further by planting a silver cup in Benjamin's satchel and pretending to threaten Benjamin when the cup is 'discovered'.

But his brothers cry out begging him not to harm the boy. Judah even offers his own life in exchange for Benjamin's. Seeing that his brother's hearts had truly changed, Joseph reveals his identity.

The sound of the family crying with joy at finding each other again, and reconciling, could be heard throughout the Pharaohs Courts.

Joseph brother's then go back to Jacob with the good news of Joseph's safety, and bring Jacob and his household to Egypt to live with Joseph. (In these chapters, Jacob is using his new name 'Israel')

Moving into chapters 48-50 ~ Jacob promises Joseph that the covenant will pass on through Joseph and his two sons, Manasseh and Ephraim.

When Jacob places his hands on the two boys to bless them, he crosses his arms, placing his right hand on Ephraim, the younger son. Jacob also prophesied over each of his sons before he died.

After Joseph buried his father Jacob in Canaan, he came back to Egypt, where his descendants (the Israelites) grew in number.

Before Joseph died, he told his family that one day (they and their descendants) were to return to the land God had promised to give to their ancestors: Abraham, Isaac, and Jacob.

When we look at the ongoing descendants that follow the Patriarchs, we find that JESUS is born from the line of Judah and King David (*who is a key figure later in The Bible and in the nation of Israel*).

This is the continuing of **His Story**: God **spoke His Promise** to Abraham, Isaac, and Jacob. These men **believed** and put their **faith** in God ~ leading to the coming of The Saviour for ALL mankind: **Jesus ~ God's Living Word ~** who became a man, to reveal God's True Heart to all, being full of 'grace and truth' (John 1:1-3 / John 1:14-18).

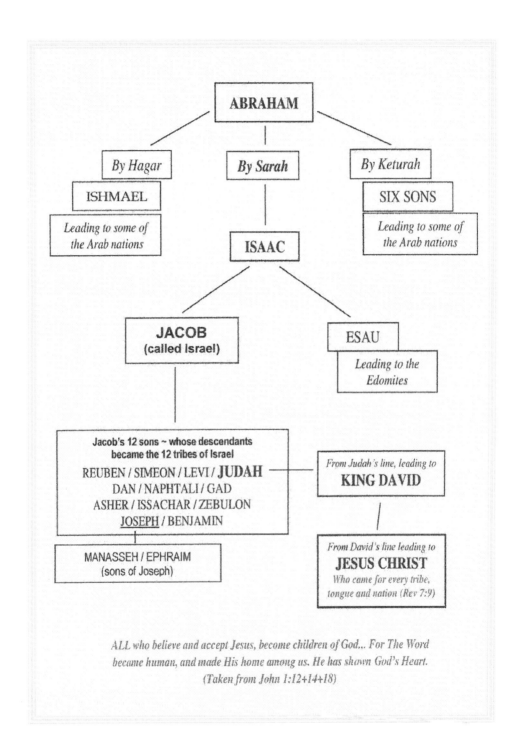

Section Six

Questions and Answers

Questions and Answers

Having looked at Genesis, here are some questions that are often asked (particularly concerning Creation) with some answers to consider:

Q1. *Could God have created the world in six days?*

A1. There is much debate about the subject of Creation. It's worth remembering that The Bible tells us 'nothing is impossible for God' (Matt 19:26 / Luke 1:37). Bearing this in mind, it could be possible for Him to create the earth in six days ~ even if this seem implausible to our own natural minds (Prov 3:5).

In the New Testament, Jesus frequently spoke to His listeners with the same notion that this is how God created the world. The Bible tells us that death and decay was not a feature of the original earth but became part of our existence as a result of the fall of mankind (Gen 3). The Apostle Paul in the New Testament also taught that creation was a supernatural event, which was then affected by suffering after the fall.

But God sent His Son Jesus to bring a solution to the need of mankind, which is the main principle that The Bible is trying to teach us. Man needed a Saviour and God sent His Son to redeem that which was lost and provide for a new heaven and earth yet to come, where death and decay will no longer have any place. As we set our hearts and minds on Him, Christ will lead us into victory in life today, in this world, as well as the everlasting to come.

Q2. *Why did God put the Tree of the knowledge of good and evil in the Garden if He didn't want them to eat of it?*

A2. It is likely that God would have one day let Adam and Eve eat from the knowledge of good and evil when they were mature enough to choose good over evil. God does not hold back anything good from His children. He wanted to keep Adam and Eve in their innocence to protect them while they matured enough to understand their authority upon the earth and say no to evil by their own free will.

Q3. *What's the big deal about eating from that tree anyway?*

A3. By doing so before they were ready they let evil take control and gave away their authority through their choice to listen to the lie of the evil one and willingly submit themselves to it. When they submitted to the wrong, and let evil in, they became controlled by sin (as would be all their descendants)

Q4. *What has God done about it then?*

A4. In Jesus, He took the authority back as a man and gave it back to mankind. All those who believe in Him have spiritual authority in Christ, to use for good not evil. That is why we need to say no to sin, not because of losing anything from God, but when we give in to it, we allow evil to reign when in fact we have the authority to kick it out.

Q5. *What about dinosaurs? Are they in The Bible and what happened to them?*

A5. Genesis chapter one tells us that people and land animals were made on the '6ᵗʰ day' of creation. Within the Old Testament pages of The Bible, large creatures are described as roaming the earth, sometimes referring to them as 'dragons' and 'sea-monsters' (for example in Job 40-41).

There are Biblical descriptions of creatures which sound 'lizard like' in nature and sometimes extremely large. These are believed to be referring to types of dinosaurs (bearing in mind that the actual name 'dinosaur' was not invented until later in the 1800s).

Many history books record details of these types of creatures all over the world, as well as many other types of animals that we do not see in our world today. The sad part is that many of them have been lost, often due to overhunting or natural disasters over the centuries.

Q6. *Who was Cain's wife?*

A6. The answer may sound unpalatable to us in today's world, but Cain would have married a sister, bearing in mind that Adam and Eve had many, many children over their long lifespans.

In the beginning, the 'original human gene pool' did not have the defects that we are aware of today, but after the fall it began to break down and so did mankind's general sense of morality.

God later gave 'covenant laws' prohibiting marriage between members of the same family later in The Bible, in order to protect mankind from the genetic consequences that would eventually follow if this was not addressed.

Q7. *If we descended from just two original people, how is DNA so complex across mankind today, giving rise to so many variations in colour of skin, hair and eyes?*

A7. The Bible tells us that God made all people and that they are descended from Adam and Eve.

Acts 17:26 (NIV)
From one man He made all the nations, that they should inhabit the whole earth; and he marked out their appointed times in history and the boundaries of their lands.

During the time of the Great Flood (Gen 6-10), eight people were saved on the great ship (Noah's Ark) that God instructed Noah to build to provide refuge for them.

The descendants of Noah's family went on to produce further descendants (all originating from Adam and Eve), which ultimately populated the world.

The colour of people's skin and the colour of people's eyes are produced by a complex system of varied genes.

To help simplify for the sake of understanding the general concept of this, we can consider how it would work IF there were just TWO GENES, which we could call A and B.

Children inherit half of their father's genes, and half of their mother's genes....

So, for analogy, let's consider the large letters 'A' and 'B' to represent the gene code for large amounts of melanin (the brown pigment that is present in everyone's skin) ~ and for comparison consider the small letters 'a' and 'b' to represent the gene code for small amounts of melanin.

In this analogy, people who have very dark skin would carry the 'AABB' genes and produce dark skinned offspring. People who have very light skin would carry the 'aabb' genes and produce light skinned offspring.

When a very dark-skinned person produces a child from a union with a light skinned person, the combination of their genes AABB and aabb would produce a child that would then carry a mix of genes AaBa (for instance) and therefore produce further children with a range of skin colour.

The same principle can be applied to eye and hair colour.

It is likely that after the division of languages at the 'Tower of Babel' (Gen 11), people would then gather together into groups who spoke the same language. These diverse groups began to separate into different lands.

Thus, we see today different people groups who have similarities to one another as they came from the same original group.

However, we also see a great variety across the globe as people groups have come together over the centuries mixing the gene pool further.

God always intended mankind to fill the earth (Gen 1:28 / Gen 9:7) but under His anointing so that the earth would be properly cared for as the population grew (Gen 2:15 / Prov 12:10).

Today, we have the opportunity to know God as He really is and be part of His Family ~ no matter what nation, tribe or tongue we may be from: man, woman and child, each one is important ~ for God loves His Creation and sent Jesus to be our Saviour.

~~~

From John 3:16-17 and John 1:12 (The Message / NLT)

"This is how much God loved the world: He gave His Son, His one and only Son..... God didn't go to all the trouble of sending His Son merely to point an accusing finger, telling the world how bad it was. He came to help, to put the world right again.... He gave the right and the power to become children of God to those who received Him (Jesus). He gave this to those who put their trust in His name.

~~~

A recommended follow up is to consider the various resources that can be found at 'Answers in Genesis' and 'Creation Ministries International' for further study if desired.

https://answersingenesis.org/

https://creation.com/

Section Seven

List and Timeline

GENESIS REFERENCE LIST

Creation (Gen 1)

The Garden of Eden (Gen 2)

The Fall of Man (Gen 3)

Cain and Abel (Gen 4)

From Adam to Noah (Gen 5)

Mankind grieves God (Gen 6)

The Great Flood (Gen 7)

The Flood Subsides (Gen 8)

Covenant of the Rainbow (Gen 9)

Noah's descendants (Gen 10)

The Tower of Babel (Gen 11)

Abram* and his household (Gen 12)

Abram and Lot separate (Gen 13)

Abram Rescues Lot (Gen 14)

God's Covenant with Abram (Gen 15)

Ishmael born to Hagar (Gen 16)

The Covenant of Circumcision (Gen 17)

God Promises Sarai** a son, Isaac (Gen 18)

Sodom and Gomorrah (Gen 19)

Abraham*, Sarah** and Abimelech (Gen 20)

Isaac Born to Sarah (Gen 21)

The Offering of Isaac (Gen 22)

Death and Burial of Sarah (Gen 23)

Isaac Marries Rebekah (Gen 24)

Jacob and Esau (Gen 25)

Isaac and Abimelech (Gen 26)

Jacob is blessed by Isaac (Gen 27)

Jacob Flees to Laban's house (Gen 28)

Jacob marries Rachel (Gen 29)

Jacob and his Sons (Gen 30)

Jacob Leaves for Canaan (Gen 31)

Jacob Wrestles with God (Gen 32)

Jacob meets Esau again (Gen 33)

Dinah is attacked (Gen 34)

Jacob named Israel (Gen 35)

Esau's descendants (Gen 36)

Joseph's sold into slavery (Gen 37)

Judah and Tamar (Gen 38)

Joseph imprisoned (Gen 39)

The Cupbearer and Baker's dreams (Gen 40)

Joseph interprets Pharaoh's dreams (Gen 41)

Joseph's brothers go to Egypt (Gen 42)

Brothers return with Benjamin (Gen 43)

Benjamin and the Silver Cup (Gen 44)

Joseph reveals his identity (Gen 45)

Jacob's household go to Egypt (Gen 46)

Jacob goes to Goshen (Gen 47)

Jacob's illness (Gen 48)

Jacob blesses his sons before he dies (Gen 49)

Death of Joseph (Gen 50)

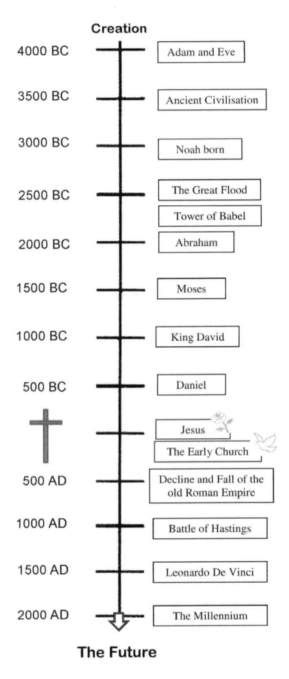

Further timeline reference notes:

By approximately 500 AD ~ the Scriptures has been translated into several languages. Writings had been copied and written down from generation to generation, copied by hand again with meticulous care to retain the work of the originals.

Around 1000 AD ~ An English Abbot (Aelfic) translated part of the Scriptures into Old English.

The printing press was invented around 1455 AD, which eventually led to the printing of The King James version of The Bible around 1600 AD.

Today (2000 AD plus) ~ Thanks to the painstaking work of so many dedicated translators, we have many versions of The Bible, in almost every language, so that people all over the world can learn from its insight.

The various translations and versions allow us to apply its wisdom into our modern world as we seek to understand (with God's help) the depths of the truth revealed through the Scriptures, as we focus on God's Love for His Creation ~ His Love for you and I.

Rom 15:4 (NIV) / 2 Thess 3:5 (GNT) from the New Testament For everything that was written in the past was written to teach us, so that through the endurance taught in the Scriptures and the encouragement they provide we might have hope..... May the Lord lead you into a greater understanding of God's love and the endurance that is given by Christ.

PERSONAL STUDY
NOTES

HIS STORY ~ Volume 1   Carmel Carberry

HIS STORY ~ Volume 1

Carmel Carberry

About The Author
And Gardenland Ministries

About the Author and 'Gardenland'

John and Carmel have an online resource of Bible Studies and Teaching Letters to offer encouragement, and share the Good News of God's unconditional love for people, whoever they are, wherever they maybe. Carmel first began to write books in 2012 when they lived in Bedford UK.

Since moving to North Derbyshire in 2018, they continue to provide free online resources on their websites and social media (please see below) and Carmel continues to write books that can be found at Amazon across the world.

GLM's foundational Scriptures: Isaiah 58:11 & Psalm 96:3 say:
"The LORD will guide you always; He will give you water when you are dry and restore your strength. You will be like a well-watered garden, like an ever-flowing spring... Publish His glorious deeds among the nations. Tell everyone about the amazing things God does!"

For more encouragement please see websites and social media links:

www.gardenlandministries.org
https://carmelcarberry.wordpress.com
www.facebook.com/groups/gardenlandministries
https://www.facebook.com/CarmelCarberry - Author
https://twitter.com/CarmelCarberry
https://www.instagram.com/carmelcarberry/

Books by the author (find at Amazon)

THE HIS STORY BOOK SERIES

His Story Volume 1 ~ looking at GENESIS

His Story Volume 2 ~ looking at THE GOSPELS

His Story Volume 3 ~ looking at ACTS and the New Testament Letters

---

GARDENLAND BOOKS

God's Fruitful Garden (a book of hope and encouragement)

Communion With God (Soaring on Eagles Wings)

SonRise (Heaven Scent)

SonSet (On The Throne)

SonDown (a taste of Heaven on Earth) ~ includes Bible Studies

Promises (Messages from God's Heart to yours)

Prayers and Blessings (Help in times of need)

Contrast (looks at Bible Covenants and the 'NEW YOU' in Christ)

Our Identity In Christ (a fresh look at our identity in Him)

Any Year Diary (with colour pictures and Bible verses)

Encouragement Notebook (notetaking journal with messages of hope)

THE ABI TAILS BOOKS SERIES

Funny stories about the family dog 'Abi' ~ with puppy pictures in full colour ~ for all ages

Abi Tails Volume 1 ~ Training my humans

Abi Tails Volume 2 ~ New Adventures

Our Beliefs at Gardenland Ministries

We believe in the authority of Scripture and that Jesus is The Living Word of God (2 Tim 3:16-17 / John 1:1+18 / Heb 1:3)

We believe in Father, Son, and Holy Spirit ~ One God manifest in three persons (Matt 28:18-19 / 2 Cor 13:14)

We believe in the death, burial and resurrection of Christ, who is now seated in Heaven at the right hand of God (1 Cor 15:3-8 / Mark 16:19-20)

We believe that anyone who puts his/her trust in Jesus is born again and becomes a new creation (Rom 10:9-13 / Rom 3:22 / 2 Cor 5:17)

We believe in the Love and Grace of God, who is full of mercy and compassion to all who come to Him (Psalm 145:8 / Eph 2:4 / Rom 8:1)

We believe in the finished work of Jesus at The Cross and that He paid for all sin for all time (Heb 7:24-25 / Rom 8:34 / Heb 4:16)

We believe that salvation includes healing (Is 53:4-5 / Luke 4:18-19 / 1 Peter 2:24)

We believe that The Holy Spirit fills and empowers believers with supernatural gifts and abilities to do good (Acts 1:8+2:4 / 1 Cor 12:7)

We believe that The Body of Christ spans across all nations and all time, united by God's eternal love (Eph 1:22-23 / Rom 12:5 / 1 Cor 12:27 / John 13:35)

YOU MATTER TO GOD

Encouragements and Prayer

A Message from God's Heart

I love you so much that I sent My one and only Son, so that through faith in Him you can receive eternal life. I did not send Him to condemn or punish you, I sent Him to rescue you.

All people everywhere have sinned, but I have demonstrated My Love for all people by sending Jesus to die on The Cross to pay for sin forever.

By faith, you can receive My free gift of salvation, for I have already provided it for you, freely by My Grace, and now you simply receive it by putting your trust in Jesus.

When you receive My Son into your heart, a spiritual new birth happens within you ~ you become My Dearly Beloved Child forever, and you become a New Creation!

As you continue to look to My Son day by day, My Holy Spirit will teach and guide you, and I will rejoice over you with singing!

With Eternal Love & Blessing
From your Heavenly Father

Related Bible verses: John 3:16-17 / Rom 3:22-24+5:8 / Eph 2:8 / John 1:12 / 2 Cor 5:17 / John 16:13 / Zeph 3:17

Please say this prayer from your heart if you would like to make Jesus Lord and Saviour of your life.....

PRAYER

Dear Lord Jesus,

Thank You that You have always loved me.

I admit that I have lived my life for myself. I am sorry and repent of my sin.

Thank You that You died on The Cross to save me. I receive the forgiveness that You earned for me.

I believe that You rose from the dead and are now seated at the right hand of The Father.

Please come into my heart to be my Lord and Saviour. Thank You that the moment I asked, You came in, to be with me forever!

Please fill me with Your Holy Spirit and empower me with good gifts to help others. To the honour of Your Name.

Amen

Welcome to the family of God!

John 1:12 (Taken from the Amplified Bible)
All who receive and welcome Him, He gives the right
[the authority, the privilege] to become children of God,
that is, to those who believe in (adhere to, trust in,
and rely on) His name

When you trust in Jesus, The Bible says these things about you....

...you are a new creation (2 Cor 5:17) you are blessed (Eph 1:3) you are God's child (John 1:12) you are redeemed (Eph 1:7-8) you are included in God's eternal plan (Eph 1:13) you have His strength and power living within you (Eph 1:19-21) you are alive in Christ and filled with God's love (Eph 2:4-6) you are seated in Heavenly places with Jesus, spiritually (Eph 2:6) you are 'hand-made' by God, His work of art (Eph 2:10) you have eternal access to God, without fear or shame (Eph 2:17-18) you are part of God's living temple, where He delights to live (Eph 2:21-22) you share in the promises of Christ as one of His heirs (Eph 3:6) you can approach God with freedom and confidence (Eph 3:12) you are being strengthened by Him in your inner being (Eph 3:16) you are loved much more than you can mentally comprehend (Eph 3:18-19) you have His power at work in you to do more than you can imagine (Eph 3:20) you are being built up and equipped for service (Eph 4:11-13) you have favour with God but He has no favourites, all are loved equally (Eph 6:9) you are strong in The Lord and His mighty power (Eph 6:10) you overcome spiritual darkness though His Light and His Word (Eph 6:12-13) you have His truth, righteousness, peace, faith, salvation, Spirit and Word to enable you (Eph 6:14-17) you have the love and peace of Christ within you, forever and for all time (Eph 6:23).

Enjoy these truths and enjoy your new relationship with God!
Please use the free resources and other helpful links that can be
*found at **www.gardenlandministries.org** to encourage*
and bless your journey with Him.

Printed in Great Britain
by Amazon